THIS BOOK BELONGS TO

_____

_____

_____

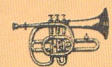

THE JOY OF
MUSIC

Musicians in the Orchestra
EDGAR DEGAS

We use music to change our emotions when we're not happy with the ones we've got. You can choose what to listen to and when and how to use this emotional repair.
John Sloboda

Music washes away from the soul the dust of every-day life.
Auerbach

The English may not like music – but they absolutely love the noise it makes.
Sir Thomas Beecham

Music is the only sensual pleasure without vice.
Samuel Johnson

Music the fiercest grief can charm,
And Fate's severest rage disarm;
Music can soften pain to ease,
And make despair and madness please;
Our joys below it can improve
And antedate the bliss above.
Alexander Pope

Music and life are one indivisible breath
expressing everything we know and feel,
from agony to love, from despair to hope.
Yehudi Menuhin

Music first and last should sound well,
should allure and enchant the ear.
Sir Thomas Beecham

After silence, that which comes nearest to
expressing the inexpressible is music.
Aldous Huxley

At the Piano
T. ROBINSON

There is music in the air,
music all around us;
The world is full of it and you simply
take as much as you require.
Edward Elgar

Country Dance
PIERRE-AUGUSTE RENOIR

Is there a heart that music cannot melt?
James Beattie

What passion cannot Music raise and quell?
John Dryden

If music be the food of love, play on…
William Shakespeare

Music is the language of the soul.

The world changes when there's music in it.
It's transformed.
Michael Tilson Thomas

Music is the medicine of a troubled mind.
Walter Haddon

The music had the heat of blood,
A passion that no words can reach;
We sat together and understood
Our own heart's speech.
Arthur Symons

There is no truer truth obtainable
by man than comes of music.
Robert Browning

Music hath charms to soothe a savage breast.
William Congreve

The function of music is to release us
from the tyranny of conscious thought.

The Orchestra Playing Mozart
RAOUL DUFY

The great musicians are the ones who can observe life…and then crystallise this down into a little tune.
Michael Tilson Thomas

Music, be it Beethoven, Bartok or the Beatles, brings us together in a sharing of sound and feeling far more than can words, while simultaneously it may reveal to us something deep within ourselves of which we had been unaware.
Yehudi Menuhin

Music is well said to be the speech of angels.
Thomas Carlyle

Without music life would be a mistake.
Friedrich Nietzsche

Musician Clowns
GINO SEVERINI

M usic is like the work of an artist
painting in sounds,
with the colour in harmony.
George Martin

Cafe Singer
EDGAR DEGAS

It is the best of all trades to make songs,
and the second best to sing them.
Hilaire Belloc

Music finds its way where
the rays of the sun cannot penetrate.
Soren Kierkegaard

Such songs have power to quiet
The restless pulse of care,
And come like the benediction
That follows after prayer.
Henry Wadsworth Longfellow

'Tis a sure sign work goes on merrily,
when folks sing at it.
Isaac Bickerstaff

The Yellow Violin
RAOUL DUFY

Life is like playing a violin solo in public
and learning the instrument as one goes on.
Samuel Butler

Music resembles poetry; in each
are nameless graces which no methods teach,
And which a master-hand alone can reach.
Alexander Pope

A few can touch the magic string,
And noisy Fame is proud to win them:
Alas for those that never sing,
But die with all their music in them!
Oliver Wendell Holmes

Music is the universal language of mankind.
Henry Wadsworth Longfellow

Musicians don't retire, they stop
when there's no more music in them.
Louis Armstrong

Of all man's creative endeavours, music
appears to be one of the most indestructible.

Music expresses that which cannot be put into words
and that which cannot remain silent.
Victor Hugo

If I were to begin life again,
I would devote it to music.
Sydney Smith

Sounds overflow the listener's brain,
So sweet, that joy is almost pain.
Percy Bysshe Shelley

The Dancing Lesson
EDGAR DEGAS

In music one must think with the heart
and feel with the brain.
George Szell

The Serenade
JULES CHERET

Music exalts each joy, allays each grief.
John Armstrong

Every day people come forward with new songs.
Music goes on forever.

Gloomy cares will be lightened by song.
Horace

He who sings scares away his woes.
Cervantes

Soft is the music that would charm for ever.
William Wordsworth

The Pensive Violinist
O. SCHOLDERER

Let my heart break with trouble:
no money jingles in my pocket, but
I play a song on my violin
and hunger and grief fall silent.
The Gypsy to his Violin

I think I should have no other moral wants,
if I could always have plenty of music.
It seems to infuse strength into my limbs
and ideas into my brain.
Life seems to go on without effort
when I am filled with music.
George Eliot

The language of tones belongs equally to all mankind,
and melody is the absolute language in which
the musician speaks to every heart.
Richard Wagner

At "Les Ambassadeurs"
EDGAR DEGAS

The song that we hear with our ears
is only the song that is sung in our hearts.
Ouida

Music is the only language in which you cannot say
a mean or sarcastic thing.
John Erskine

The hills are alive with the sound of music,
With the songs they have sung for a thousand years.
Oscar Hammerstein

Belief in the integrity of music and life,
and in the joy and vitality of making music,
reach out to us over thousands of years
of human experience.
Yehudi Menuhin

The Circus Orchestra
JEAN-FRANCOIS RAFFAELLI

Music and rhythm find their way
into the secret places of the soul.
Plato

Jazz music is to be played sweet, soft,
plenty rhythm. When you have your plenty rhythm,
with a plenty swing, it becomes beautiful.
Jelly Roll Morton

A jazz musician is a juggler who uses harmonies
instead of oranges.
Benny Green

There's sure no passion in the human soul
but finds its food in music.
George Lillo